SCHIPPER

W9-BXZ-827

MYSTERIES of the MIND

by
Joann A. Lawless

A
cpi
Book

RSVP
**RAINTREE
STECK-VAUGHN**
P U B L I S H E R S
The Steck-Vaughn Company

Austin, Texas

First Steck-Vaughn Edition 1992

Copyright © 1977 Contemporary Perspectives, Inc.

All rights reserved. No part of the material protected by this copyright may be reproduced or utilized in any form by any means, electronic or mechanical, including photocopying, recording, or by any information storage and retrieval system, without permission in writing from Steck-Vaughn Company, P.O. Box 26015, Austin, TX 78755. Printed in the United States of America.

Art and Photo Credits

Cover illustration, Lynn Sweat.
Illustrations on pages 6, 10, 14, 18, 38, 40, 45, and 46, Sam Viviano.
Photos on page 20, 28, and 29, Michal Heron/Woodfin Camp.
Illustration on page 22 and photo on page 43, Culver Pictures, Inc.
Photos on pages 26, and 39, Henry Groskinsky.
Photo on page 33, The American Museum of Natural History.
Photos on page 34 and 35, Dr. Thelma Moss.
All photo research for this book was provided by Sherry Olan and Roberta Guerrette.
Every effort has been made to trace the ownership of all copyrighted material in this book and to obtain permission for its use.

Library of Congress Number: 77-10726

Library of Congress Cataloging in Publication Data

Lawless, Joann A. 1949-
    Mysteries of the mind.

    SUMMARY: An inquiry into such phenomena as telepathic communication, healing through touch or mental powers, telekinesis, and foretelling the future.
    1. Psychical research—Juvenile literature.
[1. Psychical research] I. Title.
BF1031.L34   133.8   77-10726

ISBN 0-8172-1066-0 hardcover library binding

ISBN 0-8114-6859-3 softcover binding

18 19 20   99 98 97 96

Contents

Chapter
1

Mysteries of The Mind

In 1876, an angry editorial appeared in an American newspaper. It called for the arrest of an inventor who had taken money for a "false promise." He promised he could produce a device that would allow one person to talk to another several miles away.

"Without doubt this man is a fraud and . . . trickster," wrote the newspaper. "He must be taught the American public is too smart to be the victim of this and similar schemes."

The "trickster" was Alexander Graham Bell. The device was the telephone. Since then, tele-

WANTED!

For the taking of money under false pretenses:

ALEXANDER GRAHAM BELL

FRAUD AND TRICKSTER

He must be taught the American Public is too smart to be the Victim of this and similar schemes!

phones have been invented that enable people to communicate over thousands of miles—even light-years. Each day, scientists are finding better ways for people to talk to one another.

Today there are some people who claim to have the ability to reach people far away without using a telephone or a radio. They claim they use their *minds*! These people are called *psychics* (the Greek word *psyche* means spirit).

Psychics include housewives who claim they can predict the rise and fall of the stock market and 14-year-old twins who say they can tell what each other is doing even when they are 3,000 miles apart. There is even a six-year-old boy who says he can remember exactly what his family was like in a former life.

There are psychics who say they can do many other strange, hard-to-believe things. They claim to lift objects without touching them, predict future events, and *hear* colors. They say they can even make trips outside their bodies and communicate with the dead. There are eyewitnesses who claim to have seen these strange and mysterious powers at work.

Many scientists believe there *are* certain powers of the mind that seem magical but can be quite reasonably explained. So, don't be surprised if some of the stories in this book seem mysterious or unbelievable. Keep your mind open as you read. Perhaps you will discover that you, yourself, have some of these abilities. They may not be so strange after all!

Have you ever:
- thought about calling a friend, only to pick up the phone to find she was just calling you?

- received a "message" from a faraway friend you were "just thinking about"? Did it seem as if he *sent* you a thought over miles and miles using nothing but his mind and yours?

- felt that your pet animal needed you only to find that it had been ill while you were away from home?

These are just some examples of a form of mind power called *ESP*. ESP stands for *Extra-Sensory Perception*. Perception means "receiving information from your senses"—sight, smell, hearing, taste, and touch. But do you use your senses in the examples just described? You couldn't *see* your dog or *hear* your friend's message. ESP seems to need none of your ordinary senses.

ESP—
The Mysterious
"Sixth Sense"

ESP uses some "extra" sense we have but can't yet explain. Some of us seem to have more of this ESP than others do. The following are just a few cases of ESP that scientists have described. Can *you* explain them?

A 16-year-old girl from San Francisco was moping around the house one day. Suddenly, she "saw" a picture of her sister, Alicia, and her husband who lived in San Diego. She "saw" them in a restaurant eating dinner. The girl could tell exactly what her sister, over 400 miles away, was wearing. She "saw" a red dress with a white collar.

Alicia was startled by a tap on her shoulder.

About 15 minutes later, she got a long distance call from her sister. Alicia was calling to say she had just taken a bite of steak in a restaurant when she felt a "tap" on her shoulder. "*You leaned over*," Alicia said, "and said 'Hi' to me." Both sisters were amazed. How was this possible?

Here is a better known example of ESP. Harold Sherman, an American author and psychic, was a good friend of Sir Hubert Wilkens, the English explorer. In 1937, Sir Hubert went to the Arctic to live. He kept a diary of his experiences there. Three nights each week, he would write down his thoughts. Back in England, thousands of miles away, Harold Sherman wrote down his thoughts on each of the same nights. The two different diaries were then mailed to a third person for comparison.

Once Sir Hubert wrote, "Had a severe toothache today, and flew to Edmonton to get tooth pulled." On that very same day, Sherman wrote that he *"had a toothache!"* Sherman also wrote that he had the feeling it was really Wilkens' tooth that was hurting while he, Sherman, was feeling the pain.

Many more times their diaries matched. For example, Sherman "felt" something else happening to his friend, Sir Hubert, that appears in both diaries. Sherman somehow knew that Sir Hubert had made a forced airplane landing at Regina, Canada. "He [Sir Hubert] went to a dance in an evening dress suit," wrote Sherman. Sir Hubert later told of having borrowed a suit to go to a dance after his plane was forced down in a Canadian town.

Was it coincidence that the two men wrote the same thing in their diaries? Perhaps. But such coincidences have happened over many years to many people. There are just too many strange contacts between the minds of people to explain them as simple "coincidence."

How Sir Hubert and Sherman communicated is still a mystery, but it seems to have something to do with the fact that they were good friends. In spite of the distance between them, they felt close to each other. The strength of ESP between people may have something to do with how close their friendship is. In this case, the pain of Sir Hubert's toothache was very real to Sherman!

Two other famous people who seemed able to read each others' minds were writer Upton Sinclair and his wife, Mary. For three years they carried on ESP experiments. Mr. Sinclair would draw some picture that popped into his head. Mrs. Sinclair, in another room or as far away as 40 miles, would draw what she thought he was thinking at that moment.

Once Mr. Sinclair drew a knight's helmet. Mrs. Sinclair drew a lantern that looked very much like the helmet. The husband and wife wrote a book called *Mental Radio* in which they told of the many pictures they drew "together" while they were miles apart. *Mental Radio* may have been a good choice for their book title. Perhaps the mind can send messages across space just as radio and television send sounds and pictures through the air.

The subject of ESP has interested scientists for a long time. As long ago as 1939, Duke University set up a laboratory to test people who reported ESP experiences. The Duke scientists wanted answers to many questions. *Is ESP real? Under what conditions does the mind send and receive messages? Does everyone have ESP?*

For their ESP study, the Duke scientists made a special deck of cards with five different symbols—a star, a cross, a rectangle, a circle, and three wavy lines.

Have you ever done a card trick where you tried to guess what cards would turn up? The Duke experiment was like that. The special cards were shuffled and placed behind a screen.

The person being tested could not see them. One by one, a card was selected. The person being tested was asked to name the card.

The scientists figured that, by luck alone, a person would guess 5 cards out of 25. But some people did much better than that. They guessed so many cards that the scientists knew there had to be something more than luck at work.

A special deck of cards was created for the ESP experiments.

One young man did especially well at guessing the cards. He had a streak of 15 correct answers in a row. Later, in another test, he went on to guess 21 out of 25 cards selected. The odds against such "guessing" are over *30 billion to one*. After many such tests, the Duke scientists concluded that one out of five people tested had some ESP ability. But they still have not found out what ESP is.

Chapter
3

Can You See into Your Future?

One day, in New Mexico, an eighth-grade girl listened to her teacher read a poem. The girl's mind began to wander. She pictured herself wearing a nurse's uniform in a hospital ward. She could see one nurse—the head nurse—very clearly.

Four years later, the girl decided to go to nursing school. During her first day at the hospital, she had to report to the nurse in charge. As she walked down the hall, the hospital seemed strangely familiar. When she met the head nurse, she couldn't believe her eyes—it was the nurse in her daydream four years earlier!

Perhaps you, or someone you know, had a dream that later came true. Once a woman in Pennsylvania had a dream the night before her weekly bingo game. She dreamed that she would hit the jackpot and win $68,300. The next day, this woman was exactly $68,300 richer! After years of experiments with sleep and dreaming, scientists believe such dreams may very well be ESP at work.

The idea of ESP is certainly not new. In ancient Greece, there were people known for their ability to predict events that would happen years later. These people were called *oracles*.

Once King Croesus sent a message to all his oracles. He asked them to predict what he would be doing on a certain evening three months later. Croesus knew he would be cooking a lamb and tortoise stew in a brass pot. He thought no oracle could possibly guess such a thing.

Surprisingly, an oracle at Delphi hit the mark. She said she could even "smell" the stew the King would cook. Croesus was so amazed that he chose the woman as his trusted advisor. The oracle then predicted that a great army

To trick the oracles, King Croesus planned to cook
a delicious stew.

would be destroyed in a war Croesus was fighting at the time. The King was so pleased that he
led his soldiers proudly into battle, looking for-
ward to an easy victory. Unfortunately, it was
his army that was destroyed!

Chapter

4

The Mysteries of Sleep

Since many people say they have seen the future while dreaming, scientists have built "dream laboratories." They have asked teachers, housewives, businessmen, and students to come to the lab for their normal sleeping hours. The rooms in the dream lab are sealed off from the outside world. The people inside can only communicate with the scientists by using an intercom.

In these dream experiments, the scientists are playing the role of ESP "detectives." They aren't really interested in trying to predict future events. They want to see if a sleeping person receives ESP messages in the form of dreams.

In one dream experiment, the scientist would hold a picture and concentrate on it. The sleeping person had no possible way of seeing the picture but would try to dream of what it was. A machine was used to measure the brain's electrical activity during sleep. When the ma-

Information from the brain of the dreamer is sent by the wires of an electroencephalograph—a machine that measures electrical activity—to be recorded on a graph.

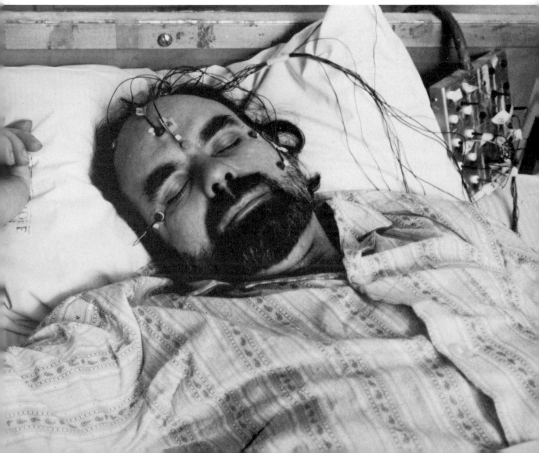

chine showed a dream taking place, the person would be awakened. The dream would then be described. One picture used in the dream study, for example, was of a boxer. The dreamer described a boxing match at Madison Square Garden!

Another picture used in the experiment was of two large dogs with white flashing teeth. They were standing over a piece of meat. Barbara, the dreamer, fell asleep quickly. The scientist held the picture outside her sealed room and thought only about those dogs and that piece of meat. Barbara was suddenly awakened by the scientist and asked to describe her dream. Barbara said, "I saw a group of greedy friends eating a rib steak. They seemed as hungry as wild dogs!"

A panel of scientists decided that, because so many of the dreams and pictures were similar, some special power of the mind had to be at work.

In another case, a dream experiment backfired. A young woman did not dream about the picture the scientist was holding. Instead, she dreamed she was in a car accident while crossing a bridge near New York City. The next morning,

she found out her boyfriend had a motorcycle accident the night before—*the night of her dream*.
The accident happened on a bridge as he was en-
tering the city! Had she been warned of his dan-
ger? Had her ESP given her a message that was
more important than a mere picture in the scientist's hand?

Abraham Lincoln believed in the power of
dreams. One week before he was killed by John
Wilkes Booth, Lincoln had a dream in which a
president was shot. Had he seen his own end?

Was Lincoln warned of his own death?

Of course, all this does not mean that if you have a bad dream it will come true. It *could* mean that at times there are powerful doses of ESP in our dreams. There is probably no better example of why ESP remains an unsolved mystery of the mind than the case of Mr. Ingo Swann. His life has been one long adventure with the unknown.

The Amazing Mind of Ingo Swann

Ingo Swann is an artist who has had amazing experiences with ESP ever since he was a child. When he was a little boy, for example, he had to have his tonsils removed. He was given a powerful drug to make him sleep. He remembers fighting to stay awake. Finally, as the doctor started the operation, Ingo Swann says he left his body. *He watched the operation take place on his body, but he was in another part of the room.*

After Ingo's operation, the nurse placed the tonsils in a container. When he recovered, Ingo asked to see them. The nurse said she had thrown them out. To everyone's surprise, Ingo told her he knew exactly where she had placed them. He told her he had seen her put them in a jar during the operation.

Swann really made a name for himself in Colorado while he was still a growing boy. He was able to help the local miners find gold ore buried deep in the hills using some mysterious "sight" he said was outside his body.

In 1973, Swann volunteered to take some tests at Stanford University in California. In the center of the laboratory at Stanford a "target" was hung from the ceiling. It was a red, heart-shaped piece of paper on a white background. Next to it was a black letter opener. But the target could not be seen from below. It was inside a box with an open lid facing the ceiling. The only way to see the target would be to climb a ladder.

For many minutes, Swann sat motionless in a chair below the box. His eyes were closed. He seemed to be thinking hard. Then he picked up a pencil and paper and calmly drew the contents of the box. He labeled each color correctly. By the end of the experiment, after

Ingo Swann sits below objects hidden from his view. He must
sense what they are.

eight different targets, Swann had scored correctly eight times out of eight!

What had Swann done to "see" the contents
of the box? He says he had what some call an *out
of body experience*. Swann says that his body
can be in one place while his senses are at
work in another. This is how his mind can see
things that are hidden from his eyes.

Swann thought it would be fun to work with someone else who seemed to have strong ESP. He chose Harold Sherman. You remember, he was the man who knew what his friend wrote far off in the Arctic. Sherman was now living in Arkansas.

In December, 1973, NASA's *Pioneer 10* was going to take pictures of Jupiter. It would be the first spacecraft to get close-up views of this planet. The two men decided to gather their own data about the planet, *eight months before the Jupiter flight!* They would compare their mental views later with pictures sent back by *Pioneer 10.*

The scenes each man "saw," one viewing from Arkansas, the other from California, were remarkably similar. When the facts came back from *Pioneer 10,* many people were amazed at the accuracy of the pictures the two had "seen."

In March, 1974, Swann and Sherman tried it again. They concentrated, this time, on the planet Mercury. They "saw" a magnetic field and a very thin atmosphere. They also "saw" a long tail of helium streaming out from the tiny planet. Again Swann and Sherman described what scientists later found to be so. The men had predicted some unusual facts about Mercury, such as the magnetic field. These were things no one could simply have guessed.

Since ancient times there have been stage performers who do tricks that appear to happen through magic. Rabbits are pulled from empty hats, people are made to disappear right before your eyes, and assistants have been cut in half by smiling magicians. Some of these performers even appear to "read" other people's minds, lift heavy objects using only "the energy of their minds," and "predict the future."

We know "mind readers" on the stage are using tricks and we applaud their talent and

A sender looks at a picture . . .

skill. We know that the moving objects are controlled, not by the performer's mind, but by thin wires or hidden machines. Many scientists are convinced that most "psychics" are also merely performing tricks. While these scientists are willing to keep an open mind, they feel there is no real evidence that anyone can "read" another's mind, "leave the body", or "see" things the eye cannot see. Nor do scientists feel anyone can lift objects into the air using only mind energy.

As Ingo Swann has been tested by scientists, so have others whom some people call psychics. A young Israeli by the name of Uri Geller was, as Ingo Swann, tested at Stanford University.

. . . A receiver tries to "see" the picture by thought alone.

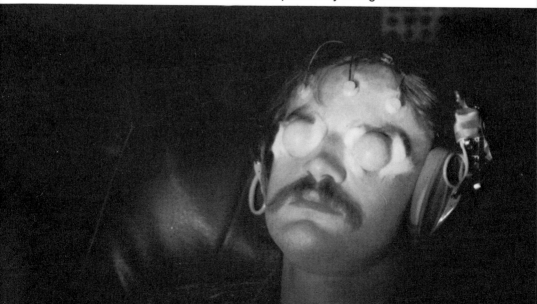

Among other mental feats, Geller appears to bend metal objects by simply *thinking* about them. In the book, "The Strange Story of Uri Geller," author Jim Collins claims that the forces of Geller's mental energy amazed scientists at Stanford. Yet, there are great numbers of people who claim that while Geller may have a brilliant mind, he has no special mental powers.

Are there people who have "psychic" powers? Can they read the thoughts of others through some special sense that gives them ESP? Do we all have some ESP we don't know how to use? Scientists continue to search for answers to these and hundreds of other questions that deal with the mysteries of the mind. Until there is more scientific evidence, however, people will continue to hotly debate about whether the Shermans and the Swanns and the Gellers are really gifted or simply very talented human beings.

Along with those who claim to have ESP, throughout history there have been people who claim to heal the sufferings of others by using the power of the mind. These *healers*, and the many people who believe in them, say they have special energy in their minds or bodies that allow them to cure the pain and illness for which most of us seek medical care.

Again, most scientists feel that there are no psychic powers that enable some to heal the bodies of others. While scientists agree that certain illnesses and problems of the mind can be cured by specially trained people (psychologists and psychiatrists), they argue that no one has the natural gift of healing diseases of the body. See what *you* think about some of the evidence people have claimed to discover in this next mystery of the mind.

Chapter
6

The Mysterious Body and Mind Healers

A set of twins, Joan and Joy, lived about 3,000 miles apart. One lived on Cape Cod, the other in the state of Washington. One day in October, Joy had a painful kidney attack. Her husband rushed her to a local hospital. At the same time, her twin sister, Joan, was on her way to a hospital because of bad back pain. As Joy got well, she became very worried about her sister.

After talking with her doctor one day about how close she and her twin sister had been all their lives, Joy wondered if just the power of her mind could stop her sister's pain. She began thinking hard about her sister Joan. When they compared notes some weeks later, the two sisters decided that when Joy began concentrating her thoughts on her sister, Joan's pain started to vanish. Whatever caused it, Joan's doctors were astonished at her sudden recovery!

Through the ages, people have claimed to possess special abilities to heal people's ailments. They don't use medicines and they have no medical knowledge. They have been called *shamans* or *medicine men* or, simply, *healers.*

An Apache medicine man at work.

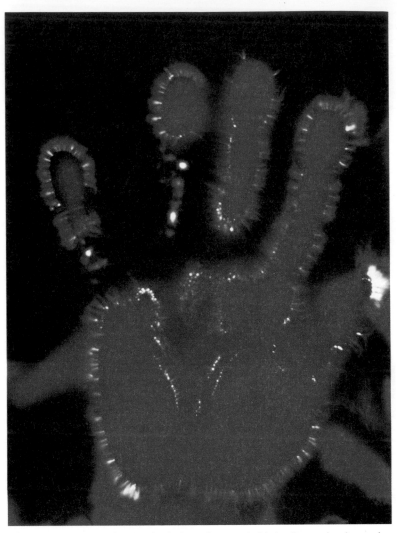

A *Kirlian* photo of a healer's hand at rest. Note the color in and around the hand. Some scientists, such as Dr. Thelma Moss, a psychologist at U.C.L.A., believe that Kirlian photos show an "energy field" around living matter. Other scientists argue that these photos are just "electrical accidents."

"Healers" have used different methods throughout the ages. Some have faced north, others, east. Some have removed all their jewelry, others have worn special jewels of copper.

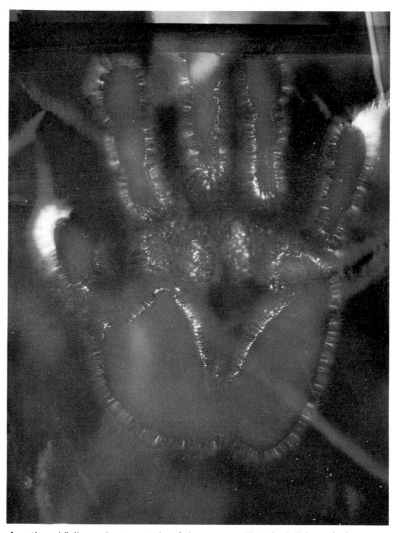

Another Kirlian photograph of the same "healer's" hand shows a change in the energy field around the hand. "Healers" might claim this is their "healing energy." Many scientists say that such changes in energy take place in all living matter and do not show any "special powers."

Whether the mind of one person has the power to heal another we do not know. But, since ancient times, mind healers have had followers who believed in them. The believers claim their pains and illnesses have been "healed" by the mind healers.

They have prayed to spirits and gods they felt would give them healing powers. Some have used their minds alone and others their hands to heal the sick. As far as can be told, healers seem to help the body repair itself. Even modern doctors, using the most advanced medicine, know the mind is important in healing the sick. A patient must be *willing* to get well.

Some healers may have *second sight*. They claim that, to them, the body is almost transparent. They are able to "see" the source of the disease. Some say they are able to spot the disease from a lock of the person's hair or from a "color" that surrounds the sick area.

Scientists have discovered that certain diseased cells of the body, such as those produced by cancer, do look different in special "heat x-ray photographs." The diseased cells seem to have a higher energy level than the healthy body cells. But no scientist has evidence that any human being can "see" such differences without using special machines invented only recently.

Chapter

7

Moving Objects with Your Mind

In a souvenir shop in Florida, many objects were breaking. Ashtrays, glasses, and mugs shot mysteriously across the floor. They fell from shelves and almost hit visitors.

One day a dagger fell from a shelf and just missed hitting a clerk. He replaced it on the shelf. A few moments later, it fell again—at a sharp angle. The clerk said it could not possibly have "fallen by itself." He felt as if it was removed by some unknown force.

The daggers fell from the shelf, just missing the clerk. Could Julio have made those knives fall just by thinking of them?

The police decided to investigate. All the accidents seemed mysteriously connected to a young boy named Julio who worked in the shop. He admitted that he was causing the mischief. He would think about an object in the shop and *it would move*. But he honestly could not explain how he did it.

All of these examples of people moving objects by mind energy are called *telekinesis*. In the 1800s, two young brothers were famous for their demonstrations of *telekinesis*. Ira and William Davenport traveled around the world demonstrating their tricks on stage. They were the sons of a policeman in Buffalo. One day at din-

Ingo Swann tries, by thought alone, to change the temperature of thermometers inside wrapped thermos bottles. Could Swann move particles of matter (atoms) simply using the energy of his mind?

ner their father noticed that the dining room table had begun to turn. He also heard raps and music which seemed to come from nowhere. His sons took credit for these puzzlers.

Soon the boys were lifting their baby sister Elizabeth from her chair—without even touching her.

Some claim that psychics can actually rise into the air just by using the energy of their own minds. Psychic D.D. Holme, an Englishman, was reported to have risen off the floor in his chair while in a trance. It is said that he was trying to contact dead spirits during a seance.

Master performers—magicians on the stage —like Harry Houdini (a famous performer of the 1920s) have done "magical" tricks that have never been understood. Heavy objects *appear* to move by themselves. Knotted ropes and locked chains seem to undo *themselves* when the magician simply thinks about them. These are all *illusions*—the performer only appears to be doing something when he really is doing something else. Most scientists feel that *telekinesis* is either just such an illusion or an accident that people imagine is caused by some mystical force.

Chapter

8

Strange Stories of the "Sixth Sense"

Once a psychologist from Latvia was recording his own voice on a tape. When he played the tape back, he noticed that it contained strange soft voices speaking in many languages. Astounded, he tried the tape again. This time the voices seemed to answer questions. He played the tape for many other scientists. All of them agreed that there were other voices on the tape. But where were the voices coming from? They seemed to speak in seven languages, the seven that the psychologist knew. No one was able to explain it.

One scientist collected 600 case histories of people who claimed they had lived other lives in the past. Such an idea is hard for most of us to believe. Yet some scientists support this belief in "other lives." They point to child geniuses. These are children who, at a very early age, show unusual gifts and skills, such as great musical ability. Yehudi Menuhin is a famous violinist who was able to play difficult symphonies perfectly when he was only five. No one had taught him this skill. Is it possible he had learned it before in another life?

Yehudi Menuhin at the age of 14. At the age of 5, he was playing symphonies.

Automatic writing is a rare ability some people seem to have. Often it does not seem to be under their control. They appear to be in a dazed or sleepy state as they write. Their arms shake violently. Some writers have composed long and beautiful poems in old languages they do not know. One woman in St. Louis who did not finish elementary school wrote historical tales from the 16th century. All her facts were accurate. Other people have written letters and messages containing facts they could not possibly have known. When these facts were checked against examples of automatic writing by other people, they mysteriously agreed.

Tina Johnson was a young American housewife. One night, as she was cooking dinner, she suddenly had the urge to grab a pencil and paper and start writing. Automatically, she began composing sentences. She recorded thoughts and feelings from distant friends, predictions, and advice to herself and her family.

Could the Tina Johnson case give us another clue to the mystery of past lives? Could her writings be out of her control? Could Tina Johnson be writing things she learned in another life?

"Automatic writers" seem to go into a trance as they write.

ESP can also help some people to enjoy music. Have you ever "seen" a picture in your mind when you listen to music? The minds of some people see colors when they hear music. When a chord is struck, they say they see a splash of color that throbs and vibrates. Some composers use this ability in writing music.

Some people see color when they hear music.

There seem to be people who "feel" what the rest of us can only *see*. Blind people are believed to be able to develop their sense of touch far beyond that of people who can see. But there is the case reported of a Russian woman with normal vision who "saw" with her hands. She could not read or write but she was able to close her eyes and "see" colors with the third and fourth fingers of her right hand. She could even tell a color when these fingers were held 12 inches above it. She never missed. She also learned to "read" numbers and words with her fingers.

Is it possible that the human mind does have a sense beyond the five we know? Can there be a *sixth* sense that gives some of us special powers to "see" things the rest of us cannot? Many people accept the idea of a sixth sense—an ESP—as the beginning of a whole new scientific frontier.

Many scientists remain doubtful, however, that most of the mysterious powers reported in this book are real. People often do imagine, or dream, things that seem so real, they accept them as fact. Perhaps it is just this way with many ESP reports. They *seem* real to the reporters, but the "powers" they witnessed can be explained simply as accidents or illusions.

Whatever the answer, we know it won't come quickly. Scientists are still having enough trouble solving even the *smallest* mysteries of the mind.